Backyard
Bird Watching
FOR KIDS

How to
Attract,
Feed, and
Provide
Homes
for Birds

By George H. Harrison

By George H. Harrison

Edited by Kit Harrison

WILLOW CREEK PRESS

Minocqua, Wisconsin

© 1997 Willow Creek Press

Published by Willow Creek Press,
P.O. Box 147, Minocqua, Wisconsin 54548

PHOTOGRAPHY CREDITS
All photographs by the author except bottom left
photo on p. 39 by Hugh Wilberg from *Hand-
Feeding Wild Birds,* Annedawn Publishing Partners.

For information on other Willow Creek titles,
call 1-800-850-WILD

Cover Design: Patricia Bickner Linder
Interior Design: Heather M. McElwain

**Library of Congress
Cataloging-in-Publication Data**

Harrison, George H.
    Backyard bird watching for kids : how to
attract, feed, and provide homes for birds / by
George H. Harrison; edited by Kit Harrison.
        p.   cm.
    Summary: Provides instructions for bird
watching and other projects involving interaction
with nature and the study of the needs and behav-
ior of wild birds.

    ISBN 1-57223-089-4 (alk. paper)
    1. Bird watching--Juvenile literature. 2. Bird
attracting--Juvenile literature. [1. Bird watching.
2. Birds--Attracting.] I. Harrison, Kit. II. Title.

QL677.5.H295   1997
598'.07'234--dc21

Printed in China

Finches fly to feeders.

Table of Contents

CHAPTER 1

Birds Are Amazing

Birds are amazing animals. Baby birds hatch from eggs by cutting their way out of the egg shells. Most are blind and without feathers when they hatch, but by the time they are a month old, they are covered with thousands of soft, colorful feathers. They eat with sharp bills, but they have no teeth. Instead, they must grind their food in a special part of their throats called a gizzard sac.

This baby crane hatched by cutting its way out of the shell with a special egg tooth located on the top of their bill.

Bird eggs come in all colors, shapes, and sizes. These are robin's eggs.

Earthworms keep these baby robins healthy and happy.

Sandhill crane in flight

The most exciting thing about birds is that they can fly. They are the largest, fastest, and most powerful fliers in the animal kingdom. A bird's feathers and honeycombed bones are so lightweight that all the bird has to do is flap its wings and it flies!

Birds are so much fun to watch that many people fix up their backyards so more birds will visit them. These people can watch birds anytime of the day, throughout the four seasons.

A father cardinal feeds insects to his babies.

Invite Them Home

You can invite beautiful wild birds to live in your backyard, too. All you have to do is give them a habitat that has the three things they need . . . cover, food, and water.

COVER   *FOOD*   *WATER*

Then, you'll be able to watch them through the windows, from inside your house. You'll see them eat, take baths, sing, build their nests, feed their babies, and even sleep.

Kids bird watching through a window

It is so easy to build a habitat for birds that everyone could be a backyard bird watcher! Just follow the directions in this book. You can make a habitat that will give the birds a safe place to live in your very own backyard.

Learning the Birds

There are lots of things you can do if you have birds in your backyard. Here are a few suggestions:

You can learn the songs and calls of the birds. You'll get to know which birds you are hearing even before you see them.

You can make a list of all the kinds of birds that live in your backyard, and mark the dates you first see them each year.

You can build bird feeders and birdhouses for the birds.

You can watch parent birds teach their babies how to crack seeds or sip sugar water. You will know what to do if a bird is injured or lost. You can even take pictures of the birds through the windows.

You may want to start a bird watching club. Then you can share your backyard bird experiences with other kids in your neighborhood or in your school.

Birds are so much fun that just watching them will make you happy! So let's get started. Let's start by identifying common backyard visitors.

CHAPTER 2

Favorite Backyard Birds

One of the wonderful things about inviting wild birds to your backyard is that so many different kinds of birds will come. And the kinds of birds will change with the seasons. On any day, during any season of the year, the average backyard habitat may contain 12 or more different kinds of birds. They will include finches, chickadees, sparrows, jays, thrushes, woodpeckers, blackbirds, doves, and maybe hawks or owls.

This chapter identifies 20 favorite backyard birds that you should be able to see in your backyard habitat sometime during the year.

 White-breasted nuthatch at nesting cavity

 Rose-breasted grosbeak at feeder

Northern Cardinal

The striking male northern cardinal is often called "redbird." He is brilliant red overall, except for a patch of black at the base of his heavy, red bill. He can raise or flatten the large red crest on his head. The lovely female is the same shape, but she is yellow-tan with red wings, crest, tail, and bill. The male's *what-cheer, what-cheer, birdie, birdie, birdie* song is a welcome sound at any time of the year. The female may call the same notes, but in a softer voice. Their forceful alarm call is a harsh *chip*. Northern cardinals are fond of sunflower seeds, cracked corn, and safflower seeds. They will also bathe and drink from birdbaths.

Eastern Bluebird

There are three kinds of bluebirds in the United States. The male eastern bluebird has a sky blue back, rusty-red breast, and white under its tail. The male western bluebird is the same, but also has a rusty-red patch on its shoulders. The male mountain bluebird is all blue with a white breast. Females are similar to their mates, but much duller. A bluebird's melodious *chur-a-lee* song is a welcome sign of spring. They live in open country on farms, along roadside fences, and at the edges of backyards. They may eat mealworms offered in tray feeders, and they often visit birdbaths, but the best way to attract them is to put up birdhouses.

Ring-necked Pheasant

Dark-eyed Junco

The male ring-necked pheasant is among the most spectacular of all birds. His bright, iridescent plumage, brilliant red face, green head, and long, tapering tail give him an elegant appearance. The less colorful female has buffy coloring and a shorter tail that helps her blend in with the dried grass where she builds her nest. In the spring, the male crows like a rooster, ending with a *whirr* of his wings. When frightened, he cackles in alarm. Pheasants live in prairies, brushy fields, and croplands. They will often visit farms and suburban backyards, where they eat seeds and cracked corn that has fallen to the ground under bird feeders.

"Snowbird" is another name for the dark-eyed junco. That's because it is most often seen in backyards when snow falls. It is a slate-gray bird with a white belly and white outer tail feathers. Juncos living in the West have a black head with a brown back and wings. Males and females look alike. The junco's spring song is a musical trill. Its winter call, or alarm note, is a simple *tic*. The dark-eyed junco is the most common songbird at North American bird feeders. It finds seeds on the ground by shuffling backwards with both feet. Its favorite habitats in winter include backyards and gardens across the continent. At bird feeders, it eats red and white millet, cracked corn, and other small grains.

Ruby-throated Hummingbird

Blue Jay

There are 15 species of humming-birds in the United States and Canada. But only the ruby-throated hummingbird lives east of the Great Plains. Males and females are like flying jewels, with iridescent, metallic green bodies. Males sport fiery-red, iridescent throats and fork-shaped tails; females have grayish white bellies and squared tails. Both utter high-pitched, squeaky, chippering calls and make buzzing noises with their wings. Any garden surrounded by trees and filled with brightly colored flowers, such as impatiens, fuschia, trumpet creeper, or honey-suckle, should attract hummingbirds. They also love sugar water.

The blue jay is a striking blue and white bird. It has a bright blue crest on its head, blue on its back, and white on its wings and tail. Males and females look alike. Blue jays are loud and noisy birds. Their demanding *jay, jay, jay* can be heard far away. Their bell-like *too-lee, too-lee* call is softer. Blue jays live in forests, farms, parks, and in the backyards and gardens of suburbs and cities. To attract blue jays, all you need to do is set up a birdbath, plus a few bird feeders containing sunflower and other bird seeds. The blue jays will come.

Black-capped Chickadee

A tiny ball of fluff with wings is the black-capped chickadee. Gray above and whitish below, the black-capped chickadee has a black cap, black bib, and white cheek marks. Males and females look the same. Black-capped chickadees say their name when they call *chick-a-dee-dee-dee!* The male's spring song is a whistled *phee-bee.* These quick-moving balls of energy are among the most curious of all backyard birds. They love sunflower seeds, both in the shell and cracked, and they can be trained to eat from your hand.

American Goldfinch

"Wild canary" is another name for the male American goldfinch. It is bright yellow with a black cap, wings, and tail, and white wing bars. The female is olive yellow with brownish-black wings and tail and white wing bars. In winter, both males and females are olive-brown. The sweet song of the male American goldfinch rises and falls like that of a canary. In flight, it calls *per-chick-a-ree.* Another call note is *see-me.* Any backyard or garden that offers water and niger or sunflower seeds is likely to attract goldfinches throughout the year.

Downy Woodpecker

Song Sparrow

A male downy is a little black and white woodpecker with a red spot on the back of its head. The female is the same, but has no red spot. A high-pitched *whinny* is their alarm note, and a contented *pik* is their feeding call. Downies live in open woodlands, orchards, swamps, and wooded backyards. A downy hunts for food while clinging to a tree trunk with its feet and pecking the tree with its bill. It is searching for insects, insect eggs, and cocoons. Of all the woodpeckers, the downy is the most common visitor to backyards. It likes suet, cracked sunflower seeds, and cracked corn.

The song sparrow is among the most common of all sparrows. It has a brown back and its heavily brown-streaked breast has a large brown spot in the center. Males and females look alike. The bird gets its name from its lovely spring song. It begins with two ringing notes, *sweet, sweet,* and then bursts into a jumble of various tones. Its call, or alarm note, is a loud *chimp.* Song sparrows dip their tails as they search the ground for seeds and insects. Bird seeds at ground feeders and water in birdbaths should attract song sparrows to backyards and gardens everywhere.

Red-winged Blackbird

Baltimore Oriole

An all-black bird with red and yellow stripes on its wings is the male red-winged blackbird. It is one of the most common and best known birds in North America. Female redwings are not black and have no red on their wings. Instead, they are quite plain in their sparrowlike, brown-striped plumage. The memorable *kong-ga-ree* song of the male redwing announces spring from still-frozen marshes across the North. The birds' *chink* call, or alarm note, sounds quite demanding. Cracked corn or cracked sunflower seeds, offered in a tray feeder, should attract red-winged blackbirds even while they are nesting nearby.

The brilliant orange and black Baltimore oriole male is among the most beautiful backyard birds of summer. The less spectacular females have olive-brown backs and are burnt orange below. The male's song is a series of varying, flutelike whistles. Its alarm call is a chattering *hue-lee*. If you hang orange or grapefruit halves in the backyard, Baltimore orioles may sip the fruit's juices. They will also drink sugar water from feeders and use birdbaths for drinking and bathing. Otherwise, look for these handsome birds in orchards and shade trees, where they build their pouchlike nests.

Tufted Titmouse

White-breasted Nuthatch

The tufted titmouse is a small, mouse-like bird with a crest. It is dark gray above and light gray below, with bright black eyes. Males and females look alike. The tufted titmouse's familiar *pet-tow, pet-tow, pet-tow* call brightens any woodland. Its *day-day-day* alarm note is harsher and more demanding. Very talented with its sharp, black bill, the tufted titmouse feeds by opening moth cocoons and shells of other insect larvae and eggs. It also eats seeds and fruit found in the woodlands. At bird feeders, titmice are fond of sunflower seeds, either in the shell or cracked. They also enjoy suet on cold days.

The white-breasted nuthatch is a little blue-gray bird with a black cap, white breast, and stubby tail. It walks down the tree trunk headfirst. The white-breasted's song is a series of rapid whistles, *whit-whi-whit-whi-whi*. Its alarm note is a harsh *yank, yank, yank*. When searching for food in the winter woodlands, white-breasted nuthatches are often in the company of chickadees, titmice, and brown creepers. This "upside-down bird" has the advantage of seeing insect food in the cracks of tree bark that other birds might miss while going up the tree trunk. It is also fond of sunflower seeds and suet in bird feeders.

House Finch

Mourning Dove

The male house finch is sometimes called a "red sparrow." It has an orange-red head, bib, and rump on a brown-streaked body. Females and immatures have no red, but are heavily streaked with brown like sparrows. The lively, warbling song of both the male and female house finch is a welcome sound in most backyards. The call, or alarm note, is a sweet *queet*. The adaptable house finch was once a purely western bird, but today it thrives throughout the country. It is satisfied in many habitats, from desert to open forests, farmlands, and suburban backyards. House finches flock to backyard feeders that offer sunflower and niger seeds.

The mourning dove is a long and slender bird, smaller than a pigeon. It is gray-brown with scattered black spots and a hint of pink wash on its breast. In flight, the tail shows white edges and the wings make a whistle. Males and females look alike. The mourning dove's *coo-ah, coo, coo, coo* call sounds sad, which explains why it's named "mourning dove." The mourning dove's diet is almost entirely grain, weed, and grass seeds. In backyards, it eats cracked corn and other smaller grains in tray feeders that are on or near the ground. Its love of water also brings it to backyards where birdbaths are provided.

Northern Mockingbird

Rose-breasted Grosbeak

White patches in the wings and tail are the flashy field marks of the otherwise dull gray northern mockingbird. Males and females look alike. Named for their many different songs and noises, northern mockingbirds can imitate the songs of other birds and other noises, such as alarm clocks and whistles. Its own alarm call is a harsh *tchack.* They are famous for singing at night, particularly on warm nights when people have their windows open and are trying to sleep! Mockingbirds live in the hedges and thickets of backyards, farms, and parks. They will eat bird cakes as well as raisins and other fruit at backyard feeders. They often visit birdbaths to drink and bathe.

The male rose-breasted grosbeak really has a rose-red breast in the shape of a bib. Otherwise, it has a striking pattern of black and white overall, with a cream-colored bill. The female is so different in her brown and white stripes that the two birds don't look like they are related. The rosebreast's heavy bill is used for cracking seeds, such as the sunflower seeds it finds at backyard feeders. The male's song is similar to that of the American robin, but richer and more musical. The alarm note is a loud *chink.* Rose-breasted grosbeaks are quiet birds that sing beautifully, appear to be devoted parents, and visit feeders and birdbaths throughout the summer.

House Wren

American Robin

A little brown bird full of energy and song is the house wren. The most common wren in North America, the house wren is dark brown above and light brown below. Males and females look alike. The bubbling, chattering song of the male rises and then falls at the end. When house wrens scold, they make a *zzzzzzsssszzz* sound. House wrens will build their nest of sticks in a birdhouse built just for them. Several birdhouses placed in a backyard may be used by the wrens. The male wren often builds dummy nests in the extra houses to keep other wrens away.

Perhaps the favorite of all backyard birds is the American robin. Known best for its brick-red breast, the robin also has a slate gray back and yellow bill. Females are slightly paler than males. The male robin's caroling *cheer-o-lee, cheer-o-lee, cheer-o-lee* song is a welcome sound in backyards and gardens across the continent. Their *tut, tut, tut* alarm notes may sound angry. Though their diet is largely earthworms, robins also eat insects, berries, and other fruits. During early spring, American robins may eat fruit, suet, mealworms, and cracked sunflower seeds placed on or near the ground.

CHAPTER 3

Planting for Birds

T he best backyard habitats for birds have lots of cover. That usually means greenery, like trees, shrubs, and flowers. Birds like to hide in the greenery if a predator like a hawk or cat comes to the yard looking for dinner!

Birds also use the greenery like we use an umbrella. It helps keep them dry and warm when it rains or snows.

⇦ Kids planting wildlife habitat

Wildlife habitat planted around the house will bring birds up close. ⇨ ⇧

Draw a Plan

To make a backyard habitat for the birds, think about how much greenery you already have in your backyard. Then think about how much more you might need.

Start by drawing a map of your backyard on page 28. It should show your house, garage, and driveway. Then draw in the trees, shrubs, hedges, vines, and flowers that are already growing in your backyard.

Plant wildflowers and vines; recycle Christmas trees.

Next decide how much greenery you need to add to your backyard and where you will plant it. Will it be one small tree? A bushy shrub? A row of shrubs? Some flowers? Do you want to plant them in containers or in the ground?

Plan to put the tallest trees farthest away from the windows. The shortest ones should be closest to the windows. That way you won't block your view of the birds when they move in. Draw the greenery and feeders you'd like to add to your yard on page 29.

Ask your parents if you can go to a lawn and garden center or to a nursery to buy the things you want to plant for the birds.

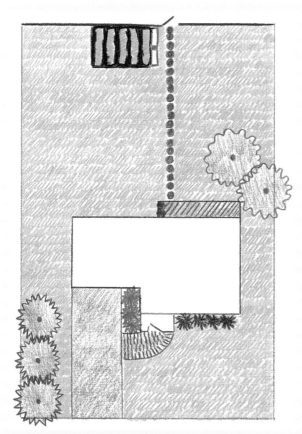

Sample of your backyard map

Wildlife habitat planted around the patio will bring birds up close.

Your backyard after adding greenery

My Yard Today
(Draw your yard here)

My Yard Improved for the Birds

Trees, shrubs, and flowers are also wonderful places for the birds to build their nests and raise their babies.

They can find some of their food in the greenery, such as insects, nuts, and berries.

Hummingbirds sip nectar from cardinal flower (left) and honeysuckle (right).

Birds Like Food Trees

If the trees, shrubs, and small plants that you choose also grow berries, fruit, or nuts, the birds will get a bonus. Not only will they find protection in the new greenery, they will find food in it, too!

Some of the plants you choose may grow in the wild in your part of the country. If so, the birds will like them even better. It will make them feel very much at home in your backyard.

When you are planting the new trees, shrubs, and flowers, be sure to carefully follow the directions for each plant. They will tell you how large a hole to dig, how deep it should be, and how much sun and water the new plants will want. Like new babies, the new greenery will need lots of care at first.

Planting may be hard work, but it will be worth it. Even a little new greenery will make a big difference for the birds. They will start to move into their new habitat in your backyard as soon as they find it!

Sunflower

Pokeberry

Crabapple

Blackberry

Nandina

Wild Grape

Dogwood

Geraniums

Wild Rose

White Oak Acorns

New Guinea Impatiens

Highbush Cranberry

Birds' Favorite Plants

	TALL TREES	SMALL TREES	TALL SHRUBS	LOW SHRUBS	PLANTS AND FLOWERS
NORTHEAST	White pine Hemlock Colorado spruce Sugar maple White and red oak Beech Birch	Flowering dogwood Crabapple Hawthorn Cherry Serviceberry Red cedar	Sumac Dogwood Highbush cranberry Elderberry Everbloom honey- suckle Winterberry Autumn olive Wisteria	Blackberry Blueberry Summer sweet Red osier dogwood Huckleberry Snowberry	Panic grass Timothy Hosta Sunflower
SOUTHEAST	Longleaf pine Loblolly pine Shortleaf pine Ash Beech Walnut Live oak Southern red oak Black gum Pecan Hackberry	Holly Dogwood Serviceberry Cherry Persimmon Red cedar Palmetto Hawthorn Crabapple	Sumac Dogwood Elderberry	Blackberry Blueberry Bayberry Spicebush Huckleberry	Panicgrass Sunflower
NORTHWEST	Douglas fir Ponderosa pine Western white pine Lodgepole pine Colorado spruce Oregon white oak California black oak Bigleaf maple	Hawthorn Serviceberry Dogwood	Sumac Bitterbrush Russian olive Elderberry Buckthorn Madrone	Blackberry Blueberry Snowberry Oregon grape	Turkeymullein Timothy Sunflower Filaree Lupine Fiddlenecks Tarweed
SOUTHWEST	Arizona cypress Piñon pine Live oak Bitter cherry	Serviceberry Dogwood Mesquite Crabapple	Mulberry Lote bush Sumac Manzanita Madrone	Utah juniper Blackberry Spicebush Prickly pear Algerita	Turkeymullein Sunflower Filaree Lupine Fiddlenecks

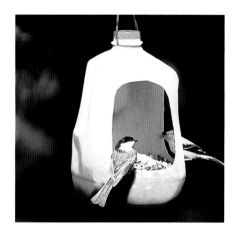

CHAPTER 4

Dinner's Ready

Feeders for the birds are like dining room tables for us. To set the table for the birds, fill the feeders with their favorite foods. The birds will fly out of the greenery to the feeders as eagerly as you come running when your favorite dinner is waiting.

Setting up bird feeders is really fun. And it's easy! Just build or buy a couple of bird feeders.

Bird feeders are easy to make out of plastic milk containers, soda bottles, pine cones, tree limbs, logs, mesh bags, and even grapefruit halves. For some of these, you might need a little help from an adult.

If you would rather buy bird feeders, visit your local wild bird store, hardware store, or lawn and garden center. You'll probably find more feeders than you can count!

 Chickadee and goldfinch use a bird feeder made from a milk bottle.

 Goldfinches eat hulled sunflower seeds at a tray feeder in winter.

Feed-a-Rama

What kinds of feeders are best for your habitat? If you give the birds several kinds of feeders, placed in different locations, you'll have more bird visitors.

Goldfinches fly to feeders

Hanging Feeders: The goldfinches, house finches, chickadees, and nuthatches like feeders that hang from a tree and blow in the wind.

Tree-trunk Feeders: Woodpeckers look for their food on tree trunks. They like a feeder filled with beef suet or bird cake. There are special bird feeders made for this. You could also put the suet or bird cake into an empty mesh bag, like onions or lemons are sold in. Hang the feeder against the tree trunk closest to your house, and you'll have woodpeckers tapping!

Kid filling beef suet feeder

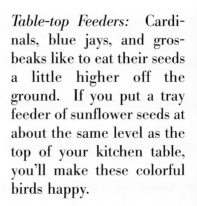

Ground Feeders: Some birds, like juncos, song sparrows, and mourning doves, like to eat on the ground. You could place a log or a wooden platform on the ground. Put it close to the window, but near some greenery. Fill it with seeds, and you'll have birds visiting almost before you can turn around!

Table-top Feeders: Cardinals, blue jays, and grosbeaks like to eat their seeds a little higher off the ground. If you put a tray feeder of sunflower seeds at about the same level as the top of your kitchen table, you'll make these colorful birds happy.

Mourning dove (above) and junco eating at ground feeders

Blue jay (above) and cardinal eating at tray feeders

Dinner Favorites

Like us, every bird has its favorite food. Many birds eat only insects. If you have lots of greenery in your habitat, there will be lots of insects for the birds to eat and to feed to their babies. The birds might also find fruit, nuts, and berries growing in your habitat. When they are hungry, they can help themselves to a snack, just like you might make a peanut butter sandwich for yourself.

Seed Eaters: Some of the most popular birds eat seeds. Seed eaters have strong, sharp bills for cracking the shells. If you serve sunflower seeds, cardinals, chickadees, and finches should flock to your feeders.

Finches love tiny black niger seeds (sometimes called thistle seeds), too. Serve them in special niger seed feeders, which are tube feeders with tiny holes.

Cardinals will gobble up safflower seeds. Juncos, sparrows, and doves enjoy cracked corn and other seeds in a wild birdseed mixture.

Suet Eaters: Woodpeckers search for insects that live on tree bark, and they like to eat suet. Give them beef suet from the supermarket meat department. Or you can give them suet cakes from wild bird stores or bird cakes that you make yourself. The woodpeckers will visit your tree trunk feeder many times a day, all year long.

Sweets for the Sweet

Sugar Water Eaters: Hummingbirds spend most of their summer days visiting brightly colored flowers, especially red ones. There, they sip nectar with their long bills.

They will also sip sugar water that you can mix for them. Stir one cup of sugar into four cups of water in a saucepan. Bring the mixture to a boil, and then allow it to cool before pouring the sugar water into a hummingbird feeder. Store leftover sugar water in the refrigerator.

Hang the feeder near bright red, pink, or orange flowers, so the hummingbirds will find it. Soon after the hummers discover the sugar water, you can move the feeder closer to the window for better viewing.

Some people add red food coloring to the sugar water, but this isn't necessary. Hummingbird feeders have some red on them so they will catch the eye of any neighborhood hummers.

Orioles have a sweet tooth, too. Try serving sugar water in a special oriole feeder. Then both the orioles and

hummingbirds can drink from the same feeder!

Watch the level of the sugar water, because the birds may soon drink it dry. If they don't finish the sugar water after three days, pour it out. Wash the feeder and refill it with fresh sugar water.

Red-bellied woodpecker eats an orange in a backyard habitat.

Fruit Eaters: Some birds, such as bluebirds, robins, woodpeckers, catbirds and mockingbirds, like to eat the same kinds of fruit that we like to eat. The rind from a grapefruit half that you have eaten makes a good bowl to put the birds' fruit in. Or you can just spread the fruit on the ground, on a platform feeder, or on a tree stump. Try pieces of apple, some raisins, berries, or orange halves. Orioles love oranges!

Kids mix sugar water for hummingbirds and orioles.

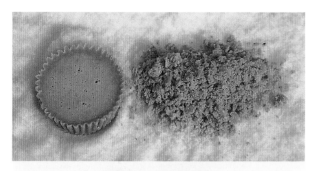

Bird Cakes

Make a cake: Lots of backyard birds like to eat bird cakes made from beef suet, cornmeal, and peanut butter. The cakes are easy to make, but you might need some help from an adult. Measure:

1 cup of peanut butter
1 cup of beef suet
6 cups of cornmeal

Melt the beef suet in a pan on the stove over low heat. Then add the peanut butter and corn meal. Mix together.

Spoon the mixture into paper-lined cupcake or muffin tins and allow them to cool. When hardened, the cakes may be removed from the tins and stored in the freezer until needed.

You could also add raisins, sunflower seeds, rolled oats, or chopped apples to your bird cake mixture. The woodpeckers, chickadees, and nuthatches will love it!

Bluebirds often enjoy mealworms, the kind that fishermen use as bait. Place the wiggly mealworms on a tray feeder.

Picky Eaters

Just as different people like different foods, different birds like different bird foods. So the more kinds of bird food you serve, the more birds will flock to your backyard habitat. However, you don't have to provide a big buffet for the birds. Just a few snacks of seeds, suet, and sugar water are okay, too. You can still have lots of fun watching birds at two or three feeders.

A Bird in the Hand

Would you like to feed birds from your hand? It takes a lot of patience, but it can be done.

When you fill the bird feeders, you may notice that some birds will come very close as you pour the seeds into the feeder. Often these will be chickadees. Chickadees are very curious, and are not as frightened of people as most of the other birds. That means they may be brave enough to take seeds that you offer in your hand.

To get started, put a chair or bench about five feet away from the feeder

Mr. Feeder Works, Too

Another way to get close to the birds while they eat is to set up a Mr. Feeder. Mr. Feeder is a dummy man that you can make. Use a plastic gallon milk jug for his head and face, put a hat on top, and give him stick arms. Put an old blanket or poncho around his shoulders and set a feeder tray in his lap.

Soon the birds will get used to eating seeds on Mr. Feeder's hat, shoulders, and lap. Then you can get dressed up like Mr. Feeder and trade places with him. Be sure to wear the same hat and cover yourself with the same blanket or poncho. If you are very still, like Mr. Feeder, the birds will eventually come in and eat from *your* hat, *your* shoulders, and the tray in *your* lap!

they use. Sit in the chair, as still as a statue, until the chickadees return to the feeder. Then move the chair a foot or two closer. Wait again for the chickadees to get used to you and to start taking seeds from the feeder.

Soon you will have moved the chair right next to the feeder. Then put some sunflower seeds on your hand. Hold out your open hand, offering the seeds to the birds. Try not to make a move! It may take a couple of weeks of moving closer and waiting an hour or so at a time before they come to you. But it will be worth it to have those tiny birds sit right on your hand. They'll be close enough for you to see their bright black eyes and every feather on their bodies.

Nuthatch and chickadee feeding

Bird Treats

Commercial suet cake

Bird Cakes (Cornmeal, peanut butter, and suet)

Beef suet

Wild birdseed mix

Beef suet

Safflower seeds

Niger (thistle) seeds

Fruit cup

Peanut butter pine cone treat

Sunflower seeds

Shishkabob

Birds' Favorite Foods

	Niger (thistle) seeds	Cracked corn	White proso millet	Red proso millet	Black oil sunflower seeds	Hulled sunflower seeds	Striped sunflower seeds
Rose-breasted Grosbeak					X	X	X
Black-headed Grosbeak					X	X	X
Evening Grosbeak		X	X		X	X	X
Northern Cardinal		X	X		X	X	X
Dark-eyed Junco	X	X	X	X	X	X	X
Song Sparrow	X	X	X	X		X	
House Sparrow	X	X	X	X	X	X	X
House Finch	X	X	X	X	X	X	X
American Goldfinch	X	X	X		X	X	X
Baltimore Oriole							
Bluebird							
American Robin						X	
Northern Mockingbird							
Hummingbird							
Tufted Titmouse	X				X	X	X
Black-capped Chickadee	X				X	X	X
White-breasted Nuthatch					X	X	X
Woodpecker					X	X	X
Blue Jay		X			X	X	X
Mourning Dove	X	X	X	X	X	X	X
Ring-necked Pheasant		X	X	X		X	

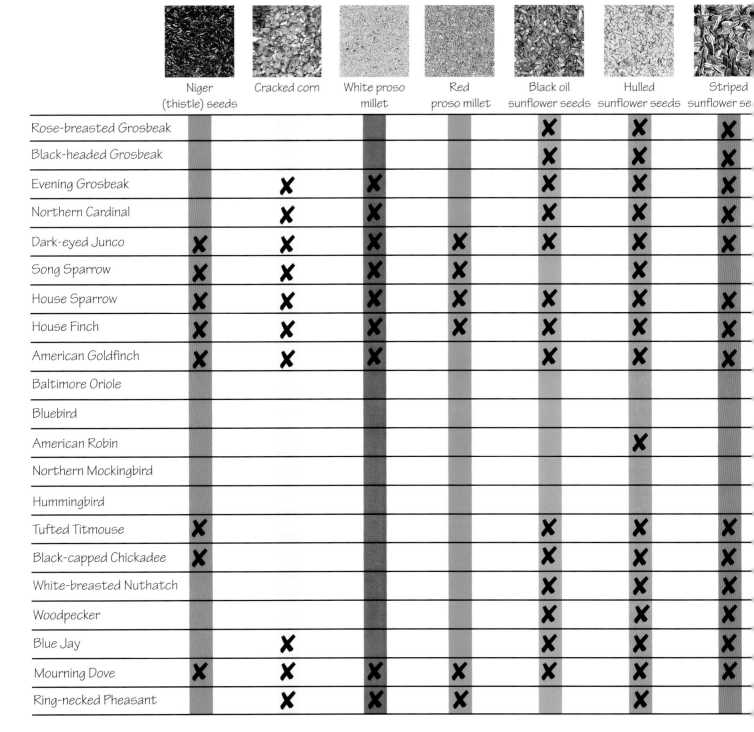

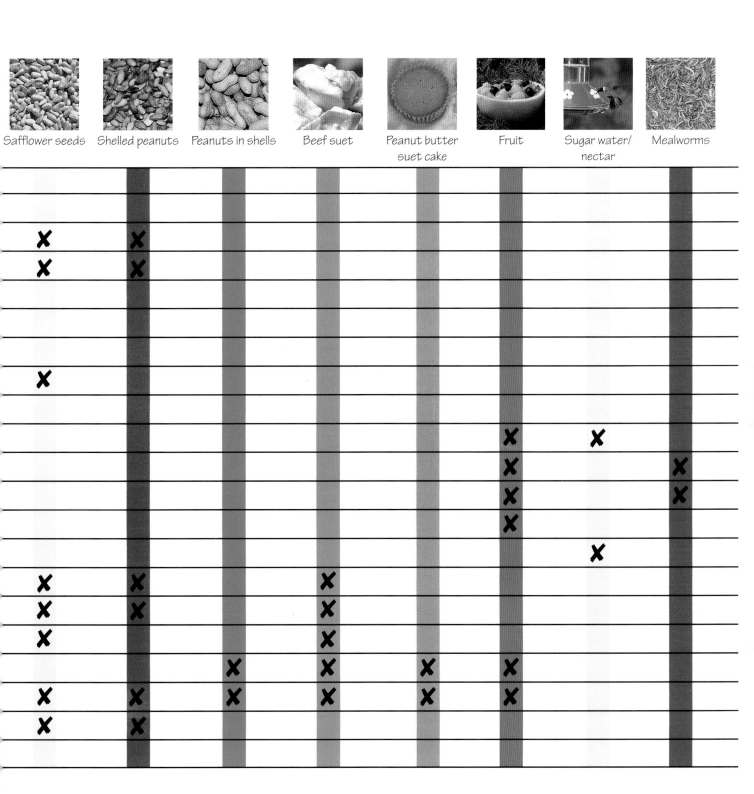

Safflower seeds	Shelled peanuts	Peanuts in shells	Beef suet	Peanut butter suet cake	Fruit	Sugar water/ nectar	Mealworms
X	X						
X	X						
X							
					X	X	
					X		X
					X		X
					X		
						X	
X	X		X				
X	X		X				
X	X		X				
		X	X	X	X		
X	X	X	X	X	X		
X	X						

Wooden Bird Feeder Instructions

These instructions are for the wooden bird feeder enclosed within this kit.

The kit includes (from top left): 2 plastic side walls; 2 roof pieces; base; 8 screws; hanger; screwdriver; foam brush; center support brace; 2 wooden side walls

Step 1) Attach the 2 wooden side walls to the base by screwing 2 screws for each wall through the pre-drilled holes in the bottom of the base.

Step 2) String the hanger through the small, center support brace.

Step 3) Attach the support brace to the 2 walls using 1 screw for each wall; make sure that the toggle nut is facing down toward the feeder base.

Step 4) Slide the 2 plastic wall pieces into place with the cut-out facing down.

Step 5) Attach the 2 sides of the feeder lid together by screwing 2 screws through the pre-drilled holes in the lid.

Step 6) String the hanger through the hole in the center of the lid and place the lid on top of the feeder.

Step 7) To fill the feeder, simply raise up the lid without removing it from the hanger.

Step 8) Hang the feeder and enjoy the birds!

Kids make bird feeders from milk bottles to hang outside their windows.

Bird feeder made from soda bottle

Bird seed scoop made from plastic bottle

CHAPTER 5

Houses for Rent

All birds need a place to build a nest. If you have lots of greenery in your backyard habitat, some of the birds will build their nests of sticks and plant fibers in your trees and shrubs. Or they might hide them on the ground under the greenery.

A few birds, such as woodpeckers, build their nests inside dead trees. They use their strong, sharp bills to hammer out a cavity in the wood. This makes a cozy nesting place for them to lay their eggs and raise their babies. That's why it's good to leave some dead trees in your habitat for these cavity-nesting birds.

If there are no dead trees in your backyard, you could put up some birdhouses. Many of the birds that make their nests in tree cavities will be happy to use birdhouses.

In fact, there are about 30 different kinds of birds that will nest in birdhouses if the houses suit them. The tiny house wren may nest in a small

⬆ *House wren in homemade house*

⬅ *Many kinds of birdhouses*

birdhouse with a 1⅛-inch entrance hole, if the house is hung in a small tree. A big wood duck may nest inside a big birdhouse with a 4-inch entrance hole. This house should be put on a tall post or on a tree close to a lake or stream.

Woodpeckers, such as flickers, red-headed woodpeckers, and red-bellied woodpeckers, may move into middle-sized birdhouses to raise their babies.

Downy woodpecker   Black-capped chickadee

Chickadees might nest in a small birdhouse placed in a wooded part of your habitat. It should be 4 to 10 feet above the ground.

Bluebirds like their houses on fence posts near a grassy field. There they will find grasshoppers, caterpillars, and flying insects to feed to their babies.

Birdhouses for tree swallows should be placed near a pond, lake, or other water.

Robins may use a half-house, or shelter, that has a roof, a floor, and one or two sides. They would build their nests of grass and mud on the floor of the shelter.

Purple martins are among the condo or apartment dwellers of the bird world. They usually nest in large, apartment-style birdhouses in which many families live under one roof. The apartment houses should be placed 25 to 30 feet above the ground, in the middle of an open, grassy lawn. That way, the martins can sweep low across the lawn to catch flying insects for their babies.

Purple martins in "condo" dwelling

Build or Buy a House

Birdhouses are easy to build. All you need are some wooden boards, a few nails, a saw, and a design to follow.

If you prefer to buy birdhouses for your habitat, visit a wild bird store, hardware store, or lawn and garden center. As with bird feeders, you will find many types of birdhouses for sale.

The best time to put up birdhouses is early in the spring. Take them down again early in the fall. Clean them out by removing any nesting material, and store them over the winter.

Baby house wrens grow up in a birdhouse.

Building a birdhouse can be fun.

Building a Bluebird House

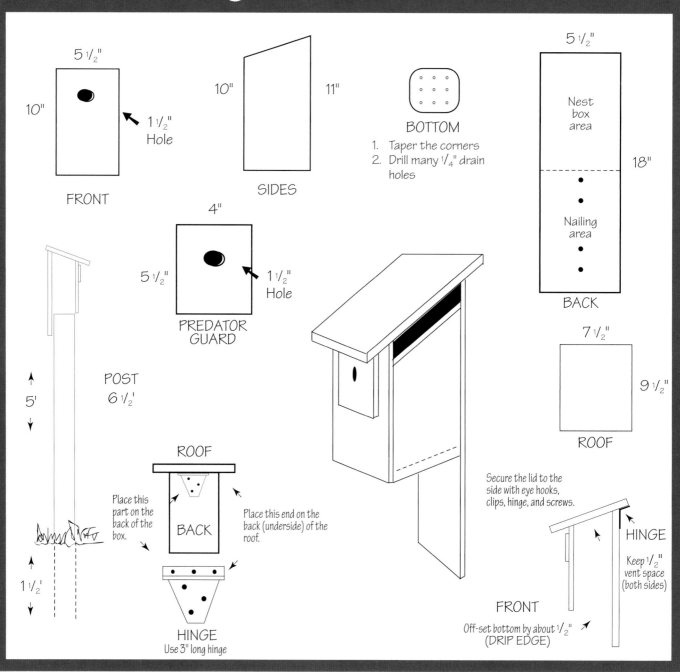

FRONT
5 ½"
10"
1 ½" Hole

SIDES
10"   11"

BOTTOM
1. Taper the corners
2. Drill many ¼" drain holes

BACK
5 ½"
Nest box area
Nailing area
18"

PREDATOR GUARD
4"
5 ½"
1 ½" Hole

POST
6 ½'
5'
1 ½'

ROOF
7 ½"
9 ½"

ROOF
BACK
Place this part on the back of the box.
Place this end on the back (underside) of the roof.

HINGE
Use 3" long hinge

Secure the lid to the side with eye hooks, clips, hinge, and screws.

HINGE
Keep ½" vent space (both sides)

FRONT
Off-set bottom by about ½" (DRIP EDGE)

Directions for Building a Bluebird House

Bluebird on homemade birdhouse

The plans for the bluebird house on the left are for a house with a top that opens. This allows you to look inside and to clean the house when you take it down for the winter.

To build this bluebird house, you need the following materials:

- Wooden boards totaling 60 inches (5 feet) long, 5½ inches wide, and 1 inch thick. Do not use treated wood; it could harm the birds.
- A wooden board 7½ inches by 9½ inches for the roof.
- One hinge, 3 inches long
- Two eye hooks for a lid
- A dozen small screws

With the help of an adult, cut the wood to the dimensions shown in the plan. Drill a 1½-inch hole in the front board and in the predator guard board. Starting with the back board, attach the sides, front, and bottom with screws. With screws or glue, attach the predator guard to help keep raccoons and other predators from reaching inside. Lastly, attach the roof with the hinge and secure with eye hooks. Paint or stain the house with a light earth color.

Place the birdhouse on a post facing an open field where the bluebirds can find insects to feed their young.

Birdhouse Specifications . . .

Tufted Titmouse

Dimensions:	4" x 4" x 8"H.
Hole:	1 1/4" hole
Placement:	4-10' high
Color:	Light earth tones
Notes:	Prefers in or near wooded area

Nuthatch

Dimensions:	4" x 4" x 10"H.
Hole:	1 1/4" centered 7 1/2" above floor
Placement:	12-25' high on tree trunk
Color:	Bark covered; natural

Tree Swallow

Dimensions:	5" x 5" x 6"H.
Hole:	1 1/2" centered 4" above floor
Placement:	5-8' high in the open, 50-100% sun
Color:	Light earth tones; gray
Notes:	Within two miles of pond or lake

Nesting Platforms

American Robin Barn Swallow Phoebe

Dimensions:	6" x 6" x 8"H.
Hole:	None
Placement:	On side of building or arbor or in tree
Color:	Light earth tones; wood
Notes:	Use is irregular

Note: With the exception of wrens, birds do not like swinging birdhouses. The houses should be firmly anchored to a post, a tree, or the side of a building.

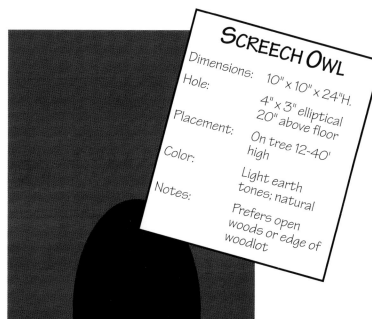

SCREECH OWL

Dimensions:	10" x 10" x 24"H.
Hole:	4" x 3" elliptical 20" above floor
Placement:	On tree 12-40' high
Color:	Light earth tones; natural
Notes:	Prefers open woods or edge of woodlot

Screech owl in wood duck house

WOOD DUCK

Dimensions:	10" x 10" x 24"H.
Hole:	4" x 3" elliptical 20" above floor
Placement:	Post 2-5' high over water or on tree 12-40' high facing water
Color:	Light earth tones
Notes:	3-4" sawdust or shavings for nesting

PURPLE MARTIN

Dimensions:	Multiple apts. 6" x 6" x 6"ea.
Hole:	2 1/2" hole 2 1/4"above floor
Placement:	15-20' high in the open
Color:	White
Notes:	Open yard without tall trees; near water

More Birdhouses To Build

BLUEBIRD

Dimensions: 5½" x 5½" x 10"H.

Hole: 1½" centered 6" above floor

Placement: 5-10' high in the open, sunny

Color: Light earth tones

Notes: Likes open areas and facing a field

HOUSE WREN

Dimensions: 4" x 4" x 8"H. or 4" x 6" base

Hole: 1⅛" centered 6" above floor

Placement: 5-10' high on post or hung in tree

Color: White; light earth tones

NORTHERN FLICKER

Dimensions:	7" x 7" x 18"H.
Hole:	2 $\frac{1}{2}$" centered 14" above floor
Placement:	8-20' high
Color:	Natural wood
Notes:	Put 4" sawdust inside for nesting

RED-HEADED WOODPECKER

Dimensions:	6" x 6" x 15"H.
Hole:	2 " centered 6-8" above floor
Placement:	8-20' high (post or tree trunk)
Color:	Natural wood
Notes:	Needs sawdust for nesting

CHICKADEE

Dimensions:	4" x 4" x 8"H. or 5" x 5" base
Hole:	1 $\frac{1}{4}$" centered 6" above floor
Placement:	4-8' high
Color:	Light earth tones
Notes:	Small tree thicket

DOWNY WOODPECKER

Dimensions:	4" x 4" x 10"H.
Hole:	1 $\frac{1}{4}$" centered 7 $\frac{1}{2}$" above floor
Placement:	12-25' high on tree trunk
Color:	Natural wood
Notes:	Prefers own excavation; provide sawdust

AMERICAN KESTREL

Dimensions:	10" x 10" x 24"H.
Hole:	4" x 3" elliptical 20" above floor
Placement:	12-40' high on post or tree
Color:	Light earth tones; natural
Notes:	Needs open approach on edge of woodlot or in isolated tree

Moving Day for Birds

When placing a birdhouse in your habitat, locate it in or near the greenery. This helps the birds feel safer while they raise their babies. Also remember to place the birdhouse so that you can watch it from your own home.

You will know when the birds are moving into the birdhouse. You'll see them carrying sticks and other nesting material into the entrance. Male house wrens may fill all the birdhouses in your habitat with sticks to keep other wrens away. These nests are called dummy nests. Only one of them will be used by the female wren to lay her eggs and raise her babies.

House wren flies to a birdhouse.

Baby house wren ready to fly

Screech owl incubating eggs in wood duck house

Female bluebird incubating eggs in birdhouse

CHAPTER 6

Watering the Birds

Without water, life on Earth would end. Birds, like people, need water to drink and water for bathing.

To care for their feathers, birds must bathe often. Then, they clean their wet feathers by combing them with their bills. Clean, healthy feathers for flying are a matter of life or death for birds.

For these reasons, water is an important part of a backyard bird habitat.

American robin taking a bath

⇧ *Evening grosbeak drinking on a cold day in winter (top)*

⇦ *Recirculating bird bath made of local stone*

Make a Bird Bath

You can give birds the water they need by setting up a birdbath. It can be as easy as putting an upside-down garbage can lid on the ground, surrounded by stones and flowers. Fill the lid with water, and watch the birds bathe and drink from it.

Or you can buy a simple, ready-made birdbath that is a shallow, round pan set on a stand.

Place the birdbath in the backyard near greenery. This location will allow the birds to feel comfortable while drinking and bathing. They'll know that they can escape into the greenery if a hungry cat or hawk appears.

The water should be changed or refreshed every day. The pan should be cleaned once a week with a brush. Use a hose to rinse out the birdbath after brushing, then refill it.

Running Water

Any kind of birdbath is good for birds. If you provide one with moving or dripping water, birds will like it even more.

Dripping birdbath

One way to make a dripping bird-bath is to hang a bucket of water in a tree above the birdbath. Punch a small hole in the bottom of the bucket before filling it with water. It will drip into the bath below, making a dripping sound that the birds will hear. Refill the bucket once or twice a day, or whenever it is empty.

Another kind of birdbath makes splashing noises. It has a pump in the water that sprays, sprinkles, or moves the water to a higher level. The birds will hear the splashing water from far away and come to your habitat to drink and bathe in it. Wild bird stores and garden centers will help you find a birdbath that moves water and will look lovely in your backyard.

Water in Winter

By heating the water in the bird-bath, you can give birds water all winter long. On very cold days, the water in your birdbath may be the only water in your area that is not frozen. You can find birdbath heaters at wild bird stores and garden centers.

A purple finch takes a drink of water in winter.

Solving Bird Problems

Like people, birds sometimes have accidents and need help. When this happens, it is important to know what to do—and what not to do—to help the birds that are in trouble.

The most typical accident happens when a bird flies into a window. This may happen if the bird sees reflections of the habitat in the window and tries to fly into the reflection.

A cut-out of an owl or hawk may keep birds from flying into the window glass.

Leave baby birds like this black-capped chickadee alone.

If a bird hits the glass, it may fall to the ground below the window. If it does, the best thing to do is to leave the bird alone until it recovers. Almost all birds that hit windows survive. Usually, they are only stunned. They should recover in a few minutes, or within an hour, and fly away. If one does die, you might want to bury it in your yard.

If birds are hitting one particular window often, there are some things you can do. Cut out a couple of large pictures of flying hawks or owls and tape them to the inside of the window. Backyard birds are afraid of hawks and owls, and may not approach the window if they see the pictures. They may think the pictures are actually the big birds and fly away from them.

The Bird in the Window

Sometimes a bird hits a windows on purpose, because when it sees itself in the reflection, it thinks it's seeing another bird. A robin or cardinal that thinks it sees another bird in the window will try to chase the "other" bird away. This usually happens in spring, when birds are protecting their nesting territory.

These birds usually don't hurt themselves when they fight their own reflections. However, if you want to stop them, try hanging pictures of hawks and owls in the window. You can also cover the window with a cloth or rub soap on the glass, so that they can no longer see the "other" bird.

Lost Baby Birds

Another possible accident in the backyard bird habitat is when a baby bird falls out of its nest. The best treatment is to leave it alone so that its mother and father can care for it. Even if you do not see the parents around, it is still best to leave the baby alone. The parents may be shy, and will care for their baby after you leave. Remember, too, that it is against the law to keep wild birds as pets, even if they are sick or injured.

Baby cardinal just out of the nest

Squirrels Can Be Pests

In almost every great backyard bird habitat there are squirrels that think the bird food is just for them. They climb up on the bird feeders, eat all the seed, and frighten the birds away. Sometimes the squirrels will even chew holes in the feeders, causing the bird food to spill out on the ground.

What can we do about these pesky squirrels?

One way to keep the squirrels off bird feeders is to give them their own feeder. Put a platform feeder near the ground, or use a tree stump and scatter corn or sunflower seeds across it. This will usually keep the squirrels happy.

Another way to keep the squirrels off post-mounted bird feeders is to use something called a squirrel baffle. This is usually a round tube, disk, or dome. It goes on top of the post, but under the feeder. A climbing squirrel cannot get around the tube or disk, so it cannot get to the feeder. Squirrel baffles will work only if the feeder is high enough off the ground—and far enough from a tree—so squirrels cannot jump over the baffle to get to the feeder.

A plastic hood above hanging feeders may keep squirrels away from the food.

Squirrels can be destructive as they climb on bird feeders and chew their way to food. A plastic baffle may keep them off.

Place food for squirrels on or near the ground to keep them off bird feeders.

Birds Will Eat Birds

One of the facts of life in the wild, and in the backyard habitat, is that every animal must eat. Sometimes this means that one animal will eat another animal in order to live. Hawks and owls are "birds of prey" that eat other birds. In addition, they eat rodents, insects, and small animals, which they also feed to their babies.

Many successful backyard habitats have one or two birds of prey living in them. Among the most common is the American kestrel. The kestrel is a small hawk that is about the size of a robin. Another is the screech owl, also a robin-sized bird. Both nest in tree cavities or large birdhouses. One of the differences between them is that the kestrel is out hunting during daylight. The screech owl hunts at night.

Don't be surprised if you see one of these birds of prey hunting for songbirds at your feeders. They are simply doing what comes naturally when they get hungry.

Seeing one bird attack another may make you feel sad for the bird that dies. Try to remember that falcons and owls have to eat, too. If it were not for birds of prey, there might be so many songbirds that there would not be enough food, cover, and water for any of them to survive. So birds of prey help to maintain the balance of nature, even in backyard habitats.

Screech owls (above), kestrels (right), and other birds of prey may visit backyard feeders in search of dinner.

CHAPTER 8

Watch the Birdie!

You'll notice right away that the birds in your backyard habitat are very beautiful. Why not take pictures of them?

Any bird worth watching on a feeder or in a birdbath is worth photographing. Imagine pictures of bright yellow goldfinches on a tube feeder . . . a brilliant red cardinal eating sunflower seeds on a tray feeder . . . a robin red-breast taking a bath . . . a baby downy

⇦ ⇧ *Photographing birds at homemade feeder*

woodpecker eating suet . . . a male blue-bird perched on top of his birdhouse.

The best way you can take these pictures is through the windows, from inside your house. The birds will not be afraid, because they cannot see you and your camera on the other side of the window. They will behave naturally while you take their picture.

Any kind of camera is fine. Hold the camera right against the window, aimed toward the birds. You can even use a flash if you keep the camera pressed tightly against the window. Hold the camera as still as possible. Wait until the birds are in a good position, then push the button without moving the camera.

You can also move the feeders around, so that each one is close to the window for a time. That way you have a better chance of taking pictures of all the birds that come to dinner in your backyard habitat.

You can take pictures through the windows of birds at feeders.

A kid's photo of a chickadee eating sunflower seeds at homemade bird feeder

You can take pictures through the windows of adult birds feeding their young.

You can take pictures of birds at birdbaths through the windows.

You can take pictures of birds that nest in houses in the backyard.

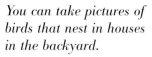

A Bird Record

If you take their pictures, you'll have a record of the birds in your habitat. Start a scrapbook, using a different page for each kind of bird (see examples on next page). Next to the pictures, you can write the date the pictures were taken and how many of the birds you saw. For example: *May 22, 1997, 15 American goldfinches eating sunflower seeds.*

Pictures of birds in the backyard can also be turned into lovely Christmas cards. Your local photo shop can use the negative from your best picture to make Christmas cards. What a hit they'll be among your friends and family!

You can set up a dummy camera at a birdhouse to get birds used to cameras.

You can also shoot videos of the birds at feeders and in the birdbath. Think how much fun it will be in the winter to look at a video of the summer birds that were in your backyard!

My Bird List

Bird Name	Date	Location	Activity
_____	_____	_____	_____
_____	_____	_____	_____
_____	_____	_____	_____
_____	_____	_____	_____
_____	_____	_____	_____
_____	_____	_____	_____
_____	_____	_____	_____
_____	_____	_____	_____
_____	_____	_____	_____
_____	_____	_____	_____
_____	_____	_____	_____
_____	_____	_____	_____
_____	_____	_____	_____
_____	_____	_____	_____
_____	_____	_____	_____
_____	_____	_____	_____

My Bird List

Bird Name	Date	Location	Activity

A Message to Adults

In our busy daily lives, which often involve work, school, sports, home care, and a myriad of other activities, there is little opportunity to enjoy the wonders of nature. Yet we all agree that exposure to the world of nature enriches our lives, and is important to the well being of our children.

The best opportunity to connect with nature on a daily basis, without leaving home, is through the wild birds that can be attracted to our backyards. That's why more and more families are developing mini nature reserves or backyard wildlife habitats in the yards immediately surrounding their houses.

By providing cover, food, and water for wild birds, adults give themselves and their children a daily link to nature. Just by looking out the window, they can see birds eating from feeders, bathing and drinking in birdbaths, protecting nesting territories, feeding youngsters, and generally behaving naturally in the habitat only a few feet away.

By involving children in efforts to make their backyards more attractive to wild birds, adults open a door of opportunity for their children to a greater understanding of our environment and a deeper love of nature—its beauty, drama, and wonder.

This book was written and illustrated in the hope that more children will make a connection with nature by attracting birds to their backyards. It presents easy to understand information and illustrations about common backyard birds. It also gives simple directions on how to attract more birds to the backyard for close-up viewing and a greater appreciation of nature than might otherwise be possible.

It is well established that children raised in homes where wild birds are an important part of daily life go on to enjoy wildlife throughout their lives. Most establish their own backyard habitats, where they and their own children continue to witness the wonders of nature just outside the window.

Caring for birds is a family affair. ⇨

"I Know My Backyard Birds"

CERTIFICATE OF RECOGNITION

After reading and identifying the birds
in Backyard Bird Watching (BBW) for Kids

_____

is an official member of the BBW Club.

CONGRATULATIONS
and keep on birding!!